KNOW
KS

JACK GILINSKY & JACK JOHNSON

HARPER

An Imprint of HarperCollinsPublishers

ALL PHOTOS COURTESY OF JACK & JACK. PHOTOS ON PAGES 37, 69, 90, 118, AND 172 BY
JSQUAREDPHOTOGRAPHY.COM. PHOTO ON PAGE 23 (TOP) BY NOEL POWELL/SHUTTERSTOCK.COM.
PHOTO ON PAGE 23 (BOTTOM) BY 1989STUDIO/SHUTTERSTOCK.COM. PHOTO ON PAGE 123 BY SONYA
ILLUSTRATION/SHUTTERSTOCK.COM. PHOTO ON PAGES 16—17, 48—49, 94—95, 106—107, AND
244—245 BY ISTOCK.COM/NATURALEDGE. PHOTO ON PAGES 79 AND 144—145 BY ISTOCK.COM/
FILIPBJORKMAN AND ISTOCK.COM/ENTERPHOTO. SPECIAL THANKS TO ANDRE LADON TURNER, CHELSEA
BLACKMAN, CALEB PHILLIPS, KABIR AFFONSO, EMMA ROYKO, SHERYL BERK, YSBNOW, FLORENT
DECHARD, THE YOUNG ASTRONAUTS, LAUREN CARROLL PHOTOGRAPHY, AND HOWARD HUANG.

LIBRARY OF CONGRESS CONTROL NUMBER: 2016939342
ISBN 978-0-06-248444-4 (TRADE BDG.)
ISBN 978-0-06-257039-0 (SPECIAL EDITION)
ISBN 978-0-06-265608-7 (SPECIAL EDITION)

TYPOGRAPHY BY BRENDA E. ANGELILLI
16 17 18 19 20   PC/RRDC   10 9 8 7 6 5 4 3 2 1
❖
FIRST EDITION

DEDICATED TO MY FAMILY—JOHN, JENNIFER, AND
JEFF JOHNSON, AND TO ALL OUR FRIENDS WHO MADE
THE MEMORIES POSSIBLE. SPECIAL THANKS TO
SHERYL BERK AND DAVID LINKER FOR HELPING US
CONFINE OUR THOUGHTS TO 256 PAGES.
—J.J.

TO THE FANS FOR MAKING OUR LIVES AND THIS
BOOK POSSIBLE
—J.G.

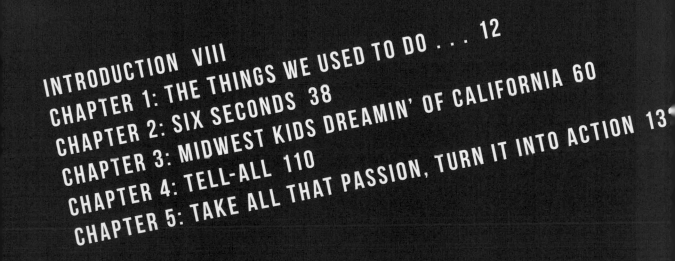

CON

TENTS

WHO ARE JACK & JACK?

G: NO, REALLY, WHO *ARE* JACK & JACK?

J: YOU'RE ASKING ME? IS THIS A TRICK QUESTION? AM I BEING GRADED? IN THE LITERAL SENSE, WE'RE JACK JOHNSON AND JACK GILINSKY.

G: TWO KIDS FROM NEBRASKA WHO MET BACK ON THE FIRST DAY OF KINDERGARTEN.

J: WE WERE A PAIR OF GOOFY KIDS, ALWAYS CLOWNING AROUND AND MAKING OUR CLASSMATES LAUGH, TRYING TO BRING A LITTLE HUMOR TO THEIR DAYS.

SO JACK & JACK ARE JUST TWO **KIDS** WHO **LOVE** ENTERTAINING **PEOPLE** IN ANY WAY, SHAPE, OR FORM—MUSIC, COMEDY, ACTING.

G: Once we matured a little bit—come fifth or sixth grade—and we started listening to music and developing our musical tastes, we discovered music was a huge part of who we are, too.

J: Right. So Jack & Jack are just two kids who love entertaining people in any way, shape, or form—music, comedy, acting. We like brightening your day. I want to have a good time, and I want everyone else to have a good time, too. Which brings us to this book that you're reading right now: party on the page.

G: When we sat down to write it, we asked ourselves: What's the message here? What do we want to say? The answer may sound a little cliché, but we just want to spread positivity.

J: I knew you were gonna say that, because that's exactly we're about.

G: And you read minds.

J: That too. We try to take our fans out of any negative places they may be in their lives and flip their mind-sets. It can be something as simple as tweeting, "Hey, keep your head up," or "Today's gonna be a great day." Don't dwell on the negative; live in the positive. And when you do, it's like a chain reaction. You spread that positivity around.

G: It's the ripple effect: someone smiles at you, smile back.

J: Growing up is hard. Being a kid is hard. Don't dwell on that. There's a lot more to life. High school is just temporary.

G: Sometimes the world feels like it's piled on your shoulders. That's when you have to let loose, enjoy yourself, and not take things so seriously.

J: I don't. Do you?

G: Never. I'm seriously never serious.

J: We also knew that in writing a book, it would help us reflect on this journey. It's giving me a better understanding of where I wanna be in life, what my future goals are, and where I wanna be next. I feel like this whole journey is leading up to something—but I don't know yet what that is.

THERE'S A LOT
MORE TO LIFE.
HIGH SCHOOL IS
JUST TEMPORARY.

G: We don't even know what we're doing next month, but we're feeling motivated to up the ante. Plus we found a ton of old photos of us from way back when.

J: We're always thinking bigger and better, and that's a great attitude to have going through life. Keep pushing yourself. This is just the beginning for us.

G: If we could do it, so can you. Who would have thought that two kids from Nebraska could make it out in Hollywood in a year and a half and get six million followers on Vine? A lot of people ask us, "How did you do it?" If you read every page, cover to cover, we promise you'll get a lot of info, a lot of inspiration, and a lot of motivation.

J: And a lot of laughs.

G: Our fans know us really well, but we want you to walk away knowing us ... well, like I know Jack.

J: He knows everything. *Everything.* It scares me a little. But our story proves the power of positivity—and also of social media. But it's true: no matter who you

are or where you are, no matter what your social or financial situation, you can make it. Seriously, you can.

G: No excuses. You got this.

J: And if you want to know who Jack & Jack are, read on. 'Cause we can't sum it all up in a few pages.

G: Definitely not. You talk too much.

J: It's been a wild ride, and we're happy to have you come along. . . .

IT'S BEEN A *WILD*
HAPPY TO HAVE YOU

RIDE, AND WE'RE COME ALONG....

"DUDE! YOU'RE WEARING THE **SAME THING AS ME?** WHAT'S UP WITH THAT?"

WHERE IT ALL BEGAN

G: WE WERE FOUR AND FIVE YEARS OLD AND IT WAS THE FIRST DAY OF KINDERGARTEN IN OMAHA. WE WALK IN, AND I DON'T THINK IT WAS IMMEDIATE, BUT I'M PRETTY SURE IT WAS IN THE FIRST HOUR OF CLASS THAT WE NOTICED EACH OTHER ACROSS THE ROOM— AND WE BOTH HAD ON THE SAME SHIRT. IT WAS THE GAP ONE WITH STRIPES ON THE ARMS; MINE WAS RED AND HIS WAS BLUE.

J: Yeah, it was like, "Dude! You're wearing the same thing as me? What's up with that?" Immediate connection.

G: Definitely some sort of connection. We had met briefly before that at a kindergarten round-up thing at a neighbor's—you know, get to know the parents, get to know your classmates.

J: But we didn't. I didn't know you, and you didn't remember me at all. I just knew at that moment on the first day that you were a kid wearing the same shirt and the same name tag.

G: Little yellow name tags that read "Jack G" and "Jack J." And that's how we were known from that day on. That's how they told us apart.

J: Wait, which one were you?

G: Ever since then, we've been best friends.

J: What if we hadn't worn those shirts? Do you think we'd be friends?

G: I never really thought about it. Maybe.

J: Wow. Scary.

G: So a shout-out to our moms for dressing us that day in those shirts. I think they picked out our clothes until second grade.

J: Wait, your mom still doesn't pick out your clothes? Hey, Mom . . . we need to have a talk!

17

⫷⫷⫷⫷ CLOWNING AROUND

J: Elementary school was definitely our biggest class-clown phase.

G: We didn't really get the real world, so we had no shame. We would just do whatever it took to make people laugh.

J: We were in time-out so much! I remember once during nap time we started tap-dancing, and our teacher, Ms. Dolphens, spun around and said, "What are you two doing?" When we explained, she was pretty cool about it. She showed the whole class a tap-dancing video.

G: It ended up being good, but I think that was partly because: a) our teacher was cool and awesome, and b) we were funny, but not in an offensive or rude way. We were just trying to have a good time.

J: During nap. Oh well. We never did have great timing.

G: When it came to recess, we were sporty. We would throw a ball around: football, basketball, kickball, foursquare, whatever. But we were never the most athletic kids. He was playing soccer, and I was doing my tennis thing.

J: Let's put it this way. If you looked at us in second grade, you would never pick us out of a crowd and say, "These two are gonna be on the varsity squad one day."

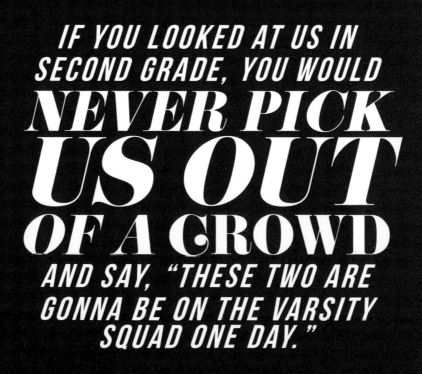

G. No. Wasn't us. We were the goofy kids.

J: The first few years we were extremely joined at the hip, during kindergarten, first grade, and second grade. But after that, we didn't have the same teacher and we weren't in the same class, so we had to expand our social circles a little. We would still hang out all the time, though. Then in sixth grade they put us back together. That was the best. Full circle.

IF YOU LOOKED AT US IN SECOND GRADE, YOU WOULD NEVER PICK US OUT OF A CROWD AND SAY, "THESE TWO ARE GONNA BE ON THE VARSITY SQUAD ONE DAY."

RITZ DIPS! YES! GOLDFISH TOO. FRUIT CHEWS, OREOS. ARE YOU GETTING HUNGRY? I'M GETTING HUNGRY.

⟨⟨⟨⟨⟨HANGIN' AND WATCHING *HANNAH*

J: If we didn't see each other all the time in school, we hung out after with the rest of our gang.

G: Literally, every day we would say, "Okay, whose house are we going to?" And we'd determine it based on who had the best snack ready to go. We knew every kid whose mom was vegan and wouldn't give us the good stuff.

J: Your mom's snack supply was decent—you always had ice-cream sandwiches. And Chex Mix was big. If someone was offering Chex Mix, we were there.

G: Yeah, we're not potato chip guys, but Chex . . .

J: And Cheez-Its—and those pretzel packs you'd dip in the fake orange cheese!

G: Ritz dips! Yes! Goldfish too. Fruit Chews, Oreos. Are you getting

hungry? I'm getting hungry. What was that thing I finished once at your house? An entire pack of those cookies from the little guys who lived in a tree?

J: The elves? The Keebler Elves? Oh man. Those dudes knew how to bake.

G: I just remember we were playing Tony Hawk video games and your mom came in and she was like, "Wait, where did all of these cookies go? Weren't there at least two dozen?" There were just crumbs. Guilty!

J: In your stomach, that's where they went. And we would watch TV. *Drake & Josh* was our fave, which is kinda weird now because we know Josh Peck. We're homies with him, and that's a little twisted if you think about it, because that was our show growing up. That was everybody's show.

G: *iCarly* too, and *That's So Raven*. Disney and Nickelodeon was it. We never needed to change the channels beyond those two. Literally you could put either of them on and we'd be into it.

J: And *Hannah Montana*. I admit it! No shame at all. I loved Hannah.

G: Occasionally we'd have to sneak off and watch *South Park* because our parents wouldn't let us.

J: Our minds started getting dirty around fifth or sixth grade. And that's when we really got big into *South Park* and when our real humor started to come out. My brother first showed it to us, and we were like, "Damn, this show is funny! Where have you been all our lives?"

G: You didn't get any of the cussing or mature stuff on Nick or Disney. Total eye-opener.

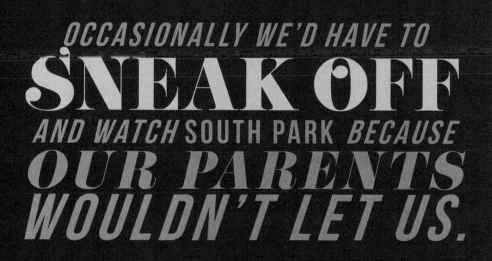

OCCASIONALLY WE'D HAVE TO **SNEAK OFF** *AND WATCH* SOUTH PARK *BECAUSE* **OUR PARENTS WOULDN'T LET US.**

AskJacks

WHAT ARE YOUR NICKNAMES FOR EACH OTHER?

G: Pretty basic: G and J.

J: Don't you mean J and G? How come you get top billing?

G: Our friends always call us that, and that's what we kind of call each other—to avoid any confusion.

J: But you're the only one who calls me Jack.

G: Yeah, because you know you're not me.

ARE OMAHA STEAKS REALLY ALL THAT?

J: Yes! Amazing. Some of the best prime. They do live up to the hype, and if you've never tasted one I strongly recommend you make it a priority.

G: I second that. Can't top those filets.

WE BOTH GO ON *AWESOME* FAMILY TRIPS AND HAVE *GREAT* SIBLINGS AND PARENTS WHO *CARE ABOUT US.*

IF YOU COULD HAVE ONE SUPERHERO POWER, WHAT WOULD YOU CHOOSE?

G: We've had this discussion many times. 'Cause you never know, one day it could happen.

J: I would teleport for sure.

G: I used to say flying or freezing time, but now I'm kinda siding with you on this. Teleportation is undeniably the best power you could have.

J: I could go anywhere I wanted, anywhere in time, and I would never have to deal with L.A. traffic.

G: So beneficial.

WHO HAS THE COOLER FAMILY? WOULD YOU EVER WANT TO TRADE?

G: Well, I'm kind of personally attached to mine, you know? I honestly couldn't tell you whose is cooler. We both go on awesome family trips and have great siblings and parents who care about us.

J: I would say we are both happy; no trading going on. Keepers.

G: That will make my mom very happy.

DID YOU GUYS HAVE TO TAKE MUSIC LESSONS WHEN YOU WERE YOUNGER?

J: Yes! I took piano lessons for eight years.

G: And I took piano for two years and drums for five. I hated going to lessons, but I liked learning new stuff. Can't have one without the other, though.

J: A good ten to twelve years of lessons between us. Shout-out to Mr. Raybine for putting up with us.

IF YOUR NAMES WEREN'T JACK & JACK, IF YOU WERE ELMO & EDUARDO INSTEAD, WHAT WOULD YOU CALL YOURSELVES PROFESSIONALLY?

J: Well, I'm glad my parents had the sense not to name me Elmo.

G: Yeah, that would be unfortunate. So what would we call our act if we were say, Travis and Donny?

J: It would have to be something cool. A band name has to be cool. Something that catches your ear.

I HATED GOING TO LESSONS, BUT
I LIKED LEARNING NEW STUFF.

G: Like Twenty-One Pilots—that's super sick. But then again, what does that mean? Are there really twenty-one of them? What if one is sick and then you're down to twenty? That's an issue.

J: I think it would have to be something very out there—like, "We are . . . Waterfall Drops."

G: I like Fiji for a name. Or They. What if we were just They?

J: I think those are both already taken. How about Truth Be Told. TBT. That's a nice band name.

G: A band name takes a lot of time and thought, so if it wasn't just Jack & Jack, if it wasn't just handed to us on a silver platter, we would be under a lot of pressure to get it right.

J: It would be a very long conversation, let's put it that way.

G: Movin' on there, Elmo . . .

A BAND NAME HAS TO BE COOL. SOMETHING THAT CATCHES YOUR EAR.

IF SOMEONE HANDED YOU A BOX FILLED WITH STUFF YOU'VE LOST THROUGHOUT YOUR LIFE, WHAT WOULD BE IN IT?

J: Multiple wallets. Multiple phones. A lot of credit cards. Tons of pairs of glasses—I just lost a pair on our trip to New York.

G: This stuffed bear named Cranberry. He might be under my bed in my home somewhere, but I'm not sure. I haven't seen him in a long time, and I miss him.

J: We had this little blue stuffed mouse, and she would definitely be in there. We took her everywhere with us one summer—Sharon was our little mascot. We went tubing at my lake house, and of course we had to keep Sharon on the tube with us, so we put her in one of our swimsuit pockets. After we got off the tube, we realized Sharon had gone MIA. We were roaming around yelling "Sharon!" searching for her.

G: As if this stuffed animal could respond. What were we thinking?

J: It was sad, man.

WE TOOK HER
EVERYWHERE
WITH US ONE SUMMER—
SHARON WAS
OUR LITTLE
MASCOT.

YOU FIGURE OUT WHAT YOU WANT AND WHAT YOU'RE GOOD AT.

SCHOOL DAZE

J: BETWEEN THE AGES OF ELEVEN AND EIGHTEEN—WHEN YOU START JUNIOR HIGH AND YOU GRADUATE HIGH SCHOOL—THAT'S A HUGE LEAP OF TIME AND GROWTH. YOUR PERSONALITY CHANGES, YOUR WHOLE VIEW ON LIFE CHANGES. YOU FIGURE OUT WHAT YOU WANT AND WHAT YOU'RE GOOD AT.

G: YOU WERE DEFINITELY SMARTER THAN I WAS. YOUR GRADES WERE BETTER. EVEN TODAY, HE'S AN OVER-ALL BRIGHTER INDIVIDUAL.

J: Gilinsky probably pulled more girls than I did. But it's a good contrast. We balance each other out.

G: As we went through high school, we were still our goofy selves, but we definitely matured. And I feel like we fit in where we fit in. There was no trying to be something we weren't.

J: Definitely. We hung with a group of cool kids, I guess you could say the popular crowd, but they weren't douchebags. They weren't the Regina Georges from *Mean Girls*.

G: Nah, everyone got along. We were lucky our school was that way. Because that's not often the case. The whole label thing ... we just avoided it. We were friends with all different types.

AS WE WENT THROUGH HIGH SCHOOL, WE WERE STILL OUR GOOFY SELVES.

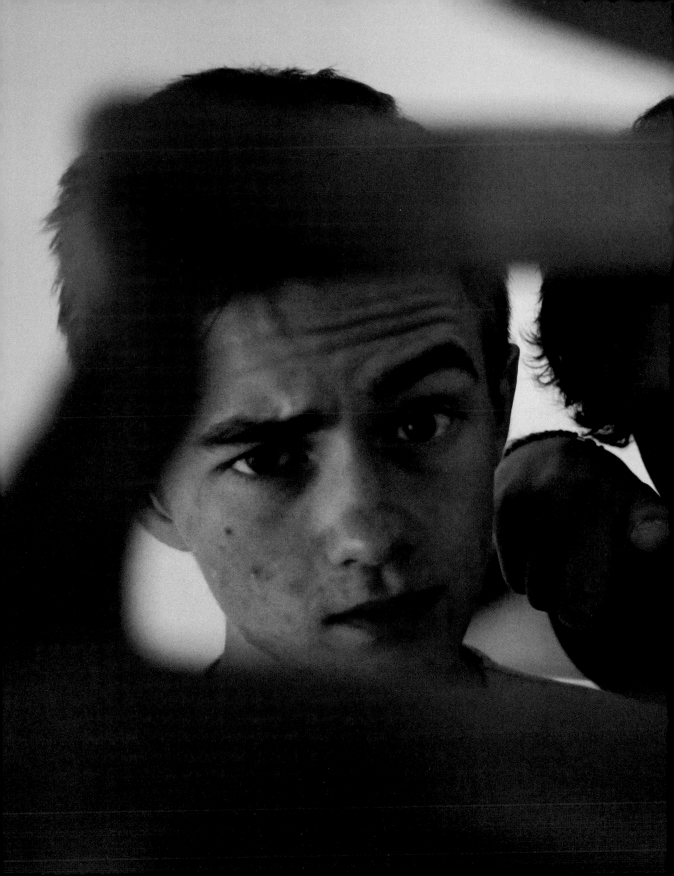

THE WHOLE **LABEL** *THING . . . WE JUST* **AVOIDED IT***. WE WERE FRIENDS WITH ALL DIFFERENT TYPES.*

<<<<<<THE FACEBOOK FEUD

G: Friends sometimes fight or go their separate ways as they grow up, but honestly, we've never gotten into an argument over anything serious.

J: What about the Facebook fight?

G: Oh yeah. There was this one time when Jack posted a photo of a kid who looked like him playing with his yellow lab on Facebook and wrote "this is my dog" and it wasn't. It wasn't him, and it wasn't his dog. I was the only one who knew it, and I wanted Jack to set the record straight.

J: It was a joke, but you were so pissed.

G: I tried to call you out on it, and you were just messing with me. You knew I was stubborn and I would keep arguing it.

J: And arguing . . . and arguing . . .

G: It was more of a joke for you, but I was actually super mad. That was a big deal for twenty-four hours, and then we were like, "Um, what are fighting about? This is stupid."

J: That's really it. That's the only time I can think of that one of us got really pissed off at the other. The rest has been silly small stuff. No fights over girls.

G: No, no. It's never over girls. Today, if we argue over anything, it's usually over business and that's wrapped up pretty quick because I'm always right.

J: Now who's joking?

G: But in general, we're pretty spot-on with each other.

J: You complete me, man.

G: Aw, I'm touched.

I TRIED TO CALL YOU OUT ON IT, AND YOU WERE JUST MESSING WITH ME. YOU KNEW I WAS STUBBORN AND I WOULD KEEP ARGUING IT.

≪≪≪≪CAN YOU SAY "AWKWARD"?

J: All through middle school, I was a hot mess.

G: We look at the old photos and we're like, "Did you guys look in the mirror before you stepped out like that? What are you wearing?" My hair was cut straight across my forehead. What's going on with that? Why didn't you tell me?

J: You think I had any clue? On any day, I was wearing like forty different colors. Don't forget you were bald at one point.

G: I was! I was a hundred percent bald. I made the summer league swim team, and I took a razor and shaved all my hair off. It was awful. I looked like a basketball.

J: I also shaved my head once. My whole soccer team did. We were supporting a teammate who had bone cancer and was going through chemo. But as for awkward, I think most people will tell you that middle school ranks up there. Although in high school, I made out with this girl that I shouldn't have. That was a tough one to live down.

I TOOK A RAZOR AND SHAVED ALL MY HAIR OFF. IT WAS AWFUL.

I THINK MOST PEOPLE WILL TELL YOU THAT MIDDLE SCHOOL RANKS UP THERE FOR MOST EMBARRASSING MOMENTS.

G: My pants fell down in chemistry class once. I had this jerky teacher, and he called me out on it. He yelled, "Gilinsky, pull your pants up!"

J: In case you didn't notice.

G: Exactly. Thanks for pointing that out.

J: Wait, what about the time with that girl at the lunch table?

G: Oh yeah. I'm changing that to my most embarrassing moment—though I covered pretty well.

J: You did.

G: My buddy Nate needed a seat, and there was this girl who always tried to sit with us and was really annoying. So I'm like, "Nate, sit here so she doesn't sit next to me! Help me out!" And I turn around and she *is* sitting next to me on the other side. I had no idea.

J: She heard it all. You looked at her and said, "Hah! Got you! You should have seen the look on your face!" As if you knew all the time she was right there.

G: Which I didn't. I think my face turned bright red, and that was the most embarrassing part: the look on *my* face when I realized what an idiot I was.

J: Yeah, that was pretty memorable. Worse than losing your pants for sure.

AskJacks

DID YOU GUYS EVER GO ALONG WITH THE CROWD—OR HAVE YOU ALWAYS MARCHED TO YOUR OWN DRUMMER?

J: There was probably a point in sophomore year of high school where I was listening to music that wasn't necessarily my taste, because all the jocks and coolest kids in the school were listening to it. I think it was humoring them more than trying to fit in.

G: Sometimes you do that for your homies. They all want to do something, and it might not be your thing but you do it—and I'm not saying bad stuff like drinking or drugs, I'm saying people wanna go to a party or a movie and you're not really up for it, but you do it anyway to be social.

J: I think you know who you are. You don't let people change that. That's just it at its simplest. You don't have to protest and be against everything everyone else does for the sake of being contrary. Be true to yourself in the most important ways, and be a team player in the others. I think that's fair, don't you?

G: Yeah, totally. Friends are important, and you want to have friends. You can be yourself without being a loner. You can be an individual and still hang with a crowd.

HOW DID YOU COME UP WITH "NERD VANDALS"?

G: "Nerd Vandals" was Jack J's idea. We would brainstorm every day, and I was kind of iffy on it for a month. He left for camp, and when he came back we sat down and put more effort into it. Then it just clicked and came together.

DO YOU GO AROUND SHARPIE-ING PEOPLE'S CARS LIKE THE NERD VANDALS?

J: To be honest, there are a few people we would have loved to . . . but no.

G: We Sharpied my car and just for the video.

WHEN WAS "THE MOMENT" YOU REALIZED YOU HAD ARRIVED? WHEN YOU WENT FROM BEING TWO NORMAL KIDS TO STARS?

J: Our first fan meet-up event in November 2013 in Dallas. It was the first time we saw our fans in person—and we saw how many of you there were. We were like, "Whoa!"

G: They picked us up in a limo at the airport. That was pretty dope. Then there were thousands of girls at the event, and a thousand girls who couldn't even get in the door. When we got back to school, people had seen the videos of fans screaming for us on the internet. Everyone was like, "Okay, this is for real." And it sunk in for us as well.

OMGLOSER2EDITS
Mar 23, 2015

Jack and Jack #4x4 #truck #LOL #funny this is nerds vandalism. #nerd4life #nerd

833 Loops

20 Likes · 12 Revines

DO YOU NEED TO WEAR DISGUISES SO YOU CAN WALK AROUND WITHOUT PEOPLE RECOGNIZING YOU?

G: Ya know, we kind of just walk around normally. We don't wear any crazy sunglasses or hats . . .

J: Yesterday, I wore a Mexican poncho that a fan gave me. With a bottle of tequila!

G: But that wasn't a disguise. It was your idea of being fashion forward.

J: True, true.

G: We don't mind being recognized. It's pretty cool, actually. Especially because we're just these two guys from Nebraska.

J: If we're in a big city, like New York, yeah, fans might stop us on the street and recognize us, ask for a photo or an autograph, and that's really great. We love it. But if we're in a smaller town, we can fly under the radar.

G: Just recently, really, it's getting a little harder to just walk into a store or the airport.

J: Yeah, but no complaints on our end. If you see a dude walkin' around in a Mexican poncho, it's me. Come say hi.

HOW TO DRESS LIKE A NERD VANDAL AND OWN IT

1. **THE BOW TIE.** Polka dot, plaid, paisley. Something with a pattern that clashes with everything else you're wearing.

2. **A PAIR OF GLASSES.** Preferably with tape across the bridge of the nose. 'Cause you broke them tripping

over your own two feet, and who has time to get new ones? Think what a librarian would wear. No fashionable shades.

3. **POCKET PROTECTOR OR FAKE ASTHMA INHALER.** The keys to Nerd Vandal accessorizing! Don't leave home without 'em. A pocket hanky or some Kleenex stuffed in the cuff of your sleeve would also be nerdlike. A nerd is always prepared if something's "snot" right.

4. **SHIRT BUTTONED TO THE TOP.** A basic white or blue button-down works, but a crazy, loud plaid is also a nice option—maybe something in a check? If it looks like a tablecloth, you're in the ballpark. Make sure the sleeves are too long.

5. **BELT OR SUSPENDERS.** Both. 'Cause a nerd needs to make sure he's not caught with his pants down, you know?

6. **SHORTS WORN HIGH ON THE WAIST.** The higher to God, the better. Seriously, if you can yank 'em up to the armpits, you're lookin' nerd chic.

7. **TALL WHITE SOCKS WITH SANDALS.** No logos or Nike swooshes. Just plain white knee socks. You could rock a pair of Vans with them, but sandals and socks are the gold standard.

8. **THE HAIR.** Combed or uncombed, it just sticks out in all the wrong directions or is shaped into a dome or combed over.

9. **THE 'TUDE.** It says, "I'm a nerd and I'm proud of it." A nerd never apologizes. He holds his head up high (almost as high as his IQ). He sees life through his four eyes and knows that he is not alone: the nerds are slated for world domination!

CHAPTER 3

MIDWE
DREAM
CALIF

HOLLYWOOD, HERE WE COME!

J: WE LEFT OMAHA TO GO TO L.A. SIMPLY BECAUSE THERE WERE JUST MORE PEOPLE HERE TO WORK WITH ON OUR MUSICAL PURSUITS. L.A. HAS THE BEST PRODUCERS AND CREATIVE TYPES, NO QUESTION ABOUT IT.

G: We were like, "Yo! We gotta get out to L.A. and take it to the next level." A few of our friends that we came up with had already moved out here. Everyone would tell us, "It's a great spot, you can't beat the weather, there are endless people doing what you wanna do." So that was it. We said, "Let's get out there ASAP!"

J: We knew if we were taking the year off before going to college, we had to be as productive as possible. The move was pretty cool. Our first week in L.A. was the most fun week of my life, just because it was all new.

G: Here, everyone is working toward something. Everyone has aspirations in the entertainment world. People have big goals, big dreams. The sky's the limit.

AskJacks
TOP FIVE THINGS WE'RE GOOD AT

1. Entertaining. Making people laugh. Getting them on their feet.

2. Putting together recreational basketball games. Calling twelve homies and saying, "Okay, we're rendezvousing here." We make it happen.

3. Making breakfast food. Eggs, bacon, toast. When we get together, we can whip up a mean morning feast.

4. Being nice. It's easy to be a jerk, but we're actually good at being kind and considerate to people. We make it our mission.

5. Answering questions. Which is prob why we started #AskJacks in the first place. We're pretty open about our lives, our likes, our screw-ups. We're really comfortable talking about ourselves, and we want our fans to feel free to ask us anything they're curious about.

PEOPLE HAVE BIG GOALS, BIG DREAMS. THE SKY'S THE LIMIT.

J: I don't think I've ever met anyone in L.A. who has an actual desk job. Everybody out here is working on their own hours, honing their craft, doing their art. The creative energy is at an all-time high.

G: We loved it from day one. It was a pretty easy transition, once we figured out the freeway and parking situations.

J: I don't know why, but I expected the food to be bad. Maybe because L.A. is so big and you hear about the smog and pollution. I thought it would be dirty.

G: Dirty food? Seriously?

J: But it's actually amazing. Great restaurants, great food. In particular, some great steakhouses and Chinese places.

G: We heard the traffic situation was awful—and that's no lie.

J: It takes twenty minutes to go a mile. In Omaha, that same distance would take you a minute, no matter what time of day. Even at rush hour.

G: There are so many aggressive drivers. Little old ladies behind the wheel will cut you off! But that's okay; I was like the only aggressive driver who lived in Omaha.

J: Overall, I would say L.A. is exactly what we expected. It's what we came here for, and I think we linked up with the right people from the jump and started making music.

G: We also weren't alone—like we said, we had a lot of friends out here who started out with us on

TOP FIVE THINGS WE SUCK AT

1. Being on time. We are at least fifteen minutes late to everything. L.A. runs on "studio time" and everyone is kinda chill with it, but honestly, we gotta work on our punctuality. It's embarrassing. If it's *Ellen*, though, we'll be on time . . .

2. Being concise. We can't answer a question in a few sentences, much less a few words. We love to ramble; we love to rant. We should probably stop ourselves there . . . or we won't shut up.

3. Cooking. We are both lacking in this department. We can maybe make a few random things, but in general, the takeout menu is our best friend.

4. Working out on a regular basis. The intentions are there, but we just can't seem to get on a schedule of going to the gym or exercising. It's really bad, we know. We always say we'll do it. It's not that we're lazy, it's just that other stuff gets in the way.

5. Getting enough sleep. Same as with working out, we mean to catch enough Zs, but there's too much to do and too few hours in the day. Also, traveling to different time zones kills us.

ALONG THE WAY, THERE HAVE BEEN PEOPLE WHO TRIED TO DISCOURAGE US.

the internet. Now they're our best, best friends—as close as our Omaha homies. They helped us and introduced us to a lot of like-minded people who keep us motivated.

«««« NO DOUBTS

J: Of course, along the way, there have been people who tried to discourage us. Haters who said, "Coming from Vine takes no talent. You might as well give up now."

G: I remember we were at our high school graduation parties and all these adults were going around asking kids, "So where you goin' next year?" It was the same story: this college, that college. But me and Jack were like, "We're movin' to L.A." Dead silence.

J: Crickets. Or "What do you mean? Why would you do that? You gotta get an education!" L.A. *is* an education.

Working in the entertainment industry *is* an education—a hands-on one.

G: That was discouraging. Because there were a lot of people who just didn't believe we could do this.

J: But we proved 'em wrong.

G: Oh yeah. But our dreams seemed so farfetched to them.

J: How many times did we hear, "You might as well go to college and take the safe route in life"?

G: Safe is boring. Maybe it's guaranteed, but it's boring.

J: Take a risk or two. If you don't do it now, the opportunity might not be there down the road.

G: You may hit traffic, but keep driving down that freeway!

J: Nice metaphor!

G: Did you catch that?

J: But seriously, on the flip side, the majority of people in our lives were positive and gave us great support. So the negative ones . . . they didn't distract us in any way, shape, or form. We knew we were gonna follow our dreams out here.

G: No doubt.

‹‹‹‹‹‹OUR BIGGEST FANS

G: Teachers, coaches, family. These were the people that believed in us the most. Mrs. Schau and Ms. Harmon, and Ms. Kleppinger, our entrepreneurship teacher. They really wanted us to go for it, to build it. Right in the beginning of senior year of high school when we started to get this following—maybe ten thousand followers—she was our biz teacher and she really encouraged us.

J: She saw the vision. She said, "You gotta take this and run with it."

G: By May and the end of her class, we had millions of followers. She said, "This is just the beginning. Follow your dream, make a lotta money."

J: Sometimes it takes just one person to tell you, "Hey, it's possible." You think your dream is crazy, and then someone comes along and says, "You're not nuts. This is real. This is possible. And it's just the tip of the iceberg if you are willing to give it all you've got."

«««« PUT DOWN THE PHONE

J: Social media is both a good and bad thing. From our perspective it's a great thing; it's our life. We wouldn't be here without it, and it allows us to connect with our fans all over the world. But on the flip side, if it invades your life and you lose touch with the real world, it's a negative. If you're not interacting with people through anything but electronic devices, that's not good. We know kids who sleep with their phones.

G: I'm not pointing a finger, but . . .

J: I don't sleep with it. Maybe it's on the nightstand *next* to my bed.

G: Social media should be used to your advantage, but it shouldn't be your priority. Not even top five. I'm on it maybe fifteen minutes a day max. When I'm bored . . .

YOU DON'T KNOW JACKS

J: When you're in the bathroom.

G: Yeah, not sure I wanted to share that—thanks, man.

J: No problem.

G: I'm not great at posting. I do it when I need to, but I don't want to get sucked into it. I've been there before, and I don't want to be there now. I've got too much going on.

J: You also have to be careful what you say or the Twittersphere will jump all over you. It's not just public personalities or celebrities that have to be careful about what they put out there, we all do. Watch your words. Words have power and they can hurt, even unintentionally. It's great to express yourself, but social media makes those words go far and fast. Think before you post.

AskJacks

WHEN WAS THE LAST TIME YOU PUT YOUR FOOT IN YOUR MOUTH?

G: Physically? I'm not sure my legs are that long.

J: When I was a kid, I used to put my foot in my mouth all the time. I bit my toenails. Once I was in sixth grade, my mom was like, "Jack, you gotta stop biting your toenails. That's just weird."

G: Okay, that's foul. I need to erase that image from my mind.

J: It's true. I mean, I bite my nails today all the time. Why are toenails any different?

G: 'Cause they're on your feet, dude!

J: Okay, but I think this question is asking in the figurative sense. In that case, I put my foot in my mouth weekly. Maybe daily. I'll see something that's negative about us online and I'll just wanna go in on them. Or sometimes, I'll

see a topic that I have a strong opinion on, and I need to say something.

G: Then you regret it.

J: Sometimes. Not always. But I'm quick to the pull that trigger, you know? If it goes against what I think and believe, I can't keep quiet.

G: I hear ya.

CAN YOU KEEP A SECRET?

G: Me, yeah. I can keep my lips zipped. Johnson . . . never. What's in his head is on his Twitter.

J: That is not true. Not entirely. Okay, maybe a little true.

G: I see you right now. You're typing, "I cannot keep a secret! #looselips."

J: Next question.

DO YOU HAVE ANY BAD HABITS?

G: Jack bites his nails. He's chowing down on them right now.

J: Jack is just perfect. He has no bad habits. It's really annoying.

G: Can I have one of yours?

J: Sure, help yourself.

DO YOU EVER EAT UNHEALTHY?

J: He eats way too many bacon cheeseburgers.

G: It's got the dairy, the protein, the carbs from the bread. I see nothing wrong with that.

J: If you say so, man.

≪≪≪TUNING IN

J: When we first started recording music, there were these two kids who went to a local high school, Turner and Travis Eakins. They were brothers, and they helped jump-start our entire musical career. They said, "Hey, we do these beats—why don't you guys come by sometime, check them out, and do some original songs." We didn't even know we could do that—write our own music?

G: That email sat in our inbox for months before we even did anything about it and met with them. We never thought we could do this. Big shout-out to the Eakinses for reaching out to us.

J: Then we went to Travis's house, and we recorded our first four songs out of this makeshift recording studio in his closet. He and Turner produced the beats, and that gave us the momentum. We sold enough copies and got some buzz going, and that gave us the marketing power to go out to L.A. It opened doors with bigger record producers.

G: It's pretty crazy. Last night we met with the guy who did "Starships" for Nicki Minaj. And the day before, a guy who worked with Ariana Grande. Who would have thought we'd ever be meeting with these hit-makers?

J: Not us. Or we would have answered Travis's email a lot sooner.

G: We work in some really cool studios now, but it started in a closet. Just sayin'.

≪≪≪≪≪HOW DID WE GET HERE?

G: Vine was our ticket, clearly. We started on Vine in July 2013 right before senior year. Before that, we were messing around on YouTube in third and fourth grade, but our friends busted on us about it, so we dropped it. Jack told me about Vine—I didn't know about it.

WE SAID, "IF WE GET TO **TWO HUNDRED FOLLOWERS,** SHOULD WE CHANGE IT TO **JACK & JACK?** " AND WE DID . . . AND WE DID!

J: We were in Lincoln, Nebraska, at this big high school convention, and all the kids there were talking about Vine, and I jumped on it. I had my own account.

G: He convinced me to do a Vine with him, and it had like sixty followers under "Jack Johnson." We said, "If we get to two hundred followers, should we change it to Jack & Jack?" And we did . . . and we did! By the time school started in August, we were grinding them out, and we had maybe twenty-five thousand followers. Our "Nerd Vandals" Vine brought us from thirty thousand to two hundred thousand in a week. We had a million by our second semester senior year. We posted every day, and a few went viral. We were addicted to watching the numbers grow. Vine was the passion at first.

J: We became the "Vine Kids." It was like the snowball effect, and before the end of the school year we had

WE CAN'T ABANDON THE
FUNNY STUFF
BECAUSE THAT'S WHERE WE STARTED,
BUT THE MUSIC
IS WHAT WE'RE FOCUSED ON NOW.

five million followers. It was a huge stepping-stone for our dream, but we never thought it would take on a life of its own. We never thought it would replace going to college. Ninety percent of what we posted were comedy videos; the rest were music covers. Then we churned out four original songs, and we realized music was the direction we wanted to take it in.

G: And it took off. We made Top 75 on iTunes with our first single, which is kinda crazy.

J: And we started to ask ourselves, what could we do if we had the right resources, the right producers, the right people in our corner? The passion kind of shifted to music. We can't abandon the funny stuff because that's where we started, but the music is what we're focused on now.

G: It wasn't out of nowhere. He was always rapping and I was always singing, and my sisters pushed me into show choir. Although we did keep that pretty quiet and understated so people wouldn't make fun of us.

J: Once we put out the first single we realized, "Hey, this is legit." I don't know when we made the final decision to not go to college and move to L.A. Probably right around May, around the college deadlines. The hardest part was convincing our parents to let us give it a shot.

G: My grades weren't great, so I think it was easier for mine to accept an alternate possibility to college. Yours were great, so your parents were probably not that eager for you to give it up.

J: We had to make them understand this could be a career for us. We could make money at it. We could be creative *and* successful. All the other kids were going to college and that had always been the game plan.

G: It is a little weird to think about that—we'd be sophomores in college now. And when we go back home and hang with our Omaha friends, college is their world. Finals and cramming and stuff. They're doing the college thing and we're not. I remember the last year of high school I was so focused on college. I wrote like seven essays, and then we didn't go.

J: Writing those college apps build character. That's how I see it.

IT IS A LITTLE **WEIRD** TO **THINK ABOUT** THAT— WE'D BE **SOPHOMORES** IN COLLEGE **NOW.**

G: Now that we're doing our music, the Vine sketch comedy thing is a little hard to put behind us. Some people don't take us seriously because of the jump.

J: But I think Vine has helped us in a huge way. We wouldn't be here without it. So no complaints for the road we've taken. Wait and you'll see. That's what I like to say to people. You wanna see what we can do, trust me, you'll see.

<<<<<<STUDIO VS. VIDEO

J: We're very visual, so the idea of making a video and translating our music into that form is really fun for us. Our roots are in video with Vine, so it's a natural for us. But that said, in the recording studio is when some of the best vibes go around. Collaborating and making something that sounds rhythmically pleasing to the ears . . . that's amazing. You can't top that.

G: I love the process as a whole, creating the music from scratch then putting a kick-ass video to it. It's fun to see it all come together. I really don't know if I could choose one part of it I like more than the other. Both are cool and creative in different ways. Both work your brain in different ways.

J: And then there's the featured stuff that we've done with Alli Simpson, Madison Pettis, Dyllan Murray. When we work with other people it's less pressure. With Alli on "Roll 'Em Up," it was kind of a doo-woppy pop vibe, and that's something we wouldn't normally do, so it gave us a chance to try new stuff. Always good to broaden your horizons.

G: It's way more chill on set when you're not the star. Which I know sounds like a crazy thing to say, because who doesn't wanna be a star? But we're actually okay with it. Sometimes it's nice to just sit back and let someone else worry about the details, you know?

J: Plenty of spotlight to go around. As much as we like to be in charge creatively of our work, it's nice sometimes to take a backseat on someone else's. And help out a friend.

G: Exactly. And you might learn a thing or two. It's good to stay open, especially in this business because you've got so many creative, talented people. Why not vibe off each other?

AskJacks

WHERE DO YOU GET INSPIRATION FOR YOUR SONGS?

G: I would say mostly from what we observe and what we experience.

J: Yeah, for example, "Wrong One" is about breaking up with a girl, how you backstab each other, and that's based on stuff we went through in high school with our girlfriends.

G: It can be based on something we experience on a day-to-day basis—or just one night out.

J: And our fans inspire us, too. "Tides" was written to lift our fans up if they're in a bad spot in life. Music can be about anything; there are no limits on what you can or can't talk about.

DID YOU GUYS EVER GET FRUSTRATED AND FEEL LIKE GIVING UP?

J: Never. The thought has never even entered my head.

MUSIC CAN BE ABOUT ANYTHING; THERE ARE NO LIMITS ON WHAT YOU CAN OR CAN'T TALK ABOUT.

G: Sometimes it's stressful, but we put it into perspective: How lucky are we to be doing what we're doing? At our age!

J: We are making music and online content for our fans, doing what we love.

G: That's why we won't ever let each other get to that point.

G: And we're really connected to our fans. A lot of what we do is for them.

J: We would never abandon our fans—we're gonna give you the same love back.

IF YOU COULD RECORD WITH ANYONE, LIVING OR DEAD, WHO WOULD YOU RECORD WITH?

J: I wish I could get Jimi Hendrix on a guitar solo on one of our songs. I just watched his documentary last night with a few buddies and it was the dopest thing ever.

G: Bob Marley. That would be sick. Someone living?

J: This guy Anderson Paak we both love and would like to work with. J. Cole on a rap track, or Bruno Mars on a funk hook.

G: Beyoncé, Adele . . .

J: Oh yeah, I didn't even think of the ladies. Of course, you would.

G: Alicia Keys. Alessia Cara.

J: Anyone who's killin' it and has a cool vibe, we'd be down for it. We love collaborating with fellow artists.

WHAT IS YOUR GO-TO KARAOKE SONG?

J: "Sweet Home Alabama." That's mine.

G: "Funky Town" maybe? Nah. Wait, I'm thinking.

J: He's thinking.

G: "The Distance" by Cake. I know, so random.

J: It's a good tune. I approve.

WHAT IS YOUR RINGTONE, AND DOES IT MATCH YOUR PERSONALITY?

J: Mine is just the factory ringtone that comes with your Apple phone. I'm too lazy to change it. And I realize that if you do pick a song, it becomes the most hated song in your brain after two weeks because you have to listen to it over and over and over again.

G: You're assuming that people call you.

J: It's like, "Damn it, not that song again!" and it just irks you.

G: It irks me too. *Irks* is a really good word, by the way.

J: Thank you. I try.

I THINK WHAT MAKES ME **LAUGH** *THE* HARDEST IS WHEN I'M NOT ALLOWED TO LAUGH.

G: I just go with the basic ring as well. What does that say about us?

J: I don't know. Maybe we're really boring. Or lame. Or indecisive.

G: Stop . . . you're irking me!

WHO—IN YOUR OPINION—IS THE FUNNIEST PERSON ON THE PLANET?

G: Jim Carrey's hilarious. Kevin Hart. Will Ferrell. Adam Sandler's a beast. It's hard to choose just one.

J: Okay, I'm picking my one person: Dave Chappelle. That's mine.

G: Then I'll go with Louis C. K. He's funny as hell. That's my choice.

WHAT JOKE/GAG MAKES YOU SHOOT MILK OUT OF YOUR NOSE?

G: Okay, wait, that actually happened.

J: I think it was in my kitchen.

G: I don't remember what you did or said, but I do remember the milk flew.

J: I think what makes me laugh the hardest is when I'm not allowed to laugh. Like you're mid-laugh and a teacher yells at you, "Stop laughing!" I can't hold it in. I lose it.

G: Jack and I used to be in the same study group with this old guy, Mr. Wish.

J: Don Wish. The man!

G: He was a veteran; he was in the war. He was intense. He tutored us in Honors Biology, and for some reason, whatever he said used to crack us up.

J: We would laugh so hard.

G: And that was bad, because he'd get mad, and when he got mad he was scary.

J: Scary but funny . . . ya gotta give Don credit.

CHAPTER 4

TERA

LOVE SONGS

J: THE EMOTIONS IN OUR SONGS COME FROM STUFF WE'VE EXPERIENCED BUT ALSO HYPOTHETICAL SITUATIONS THAT GUYS AND GIRLS EXPERIENCE. WE WANNA WRITE SONGS THAT ARE RELATABLE. THAT YOU PUT ON AND THEY TAKE YOU TO A PLACE YOU'RE AT OR AN EMOTION YOU'RE FEELING.

I DON'T THINK YOU SHOULD *EVER* KISS AND TELL.

G: In "Cold Hearted," Johnson really dove into the verses, but it's not specifically about someone we know. It's about a hot girl. You know the scenario: You encounter a really cute girl at a party or out and about. "Shallow Love" is based on a lot of stuff we've seen in L.A. People using people for fame or money. All these girls leaching on to successful guys—and vice versa—and there's nothing there. It's shallow.

J: When we wrote "Distance," we both had girlfriends and it was our first time traveling to fan events on the weekends. Weekends were big back in high school for dating; you didn't wanna miss out on the weekends. So it put stress on our relationships—the distance caused a lot of strain. We were feeling it; they were feeling it.

G: "I'm In" is about a second chance. When you and your girl break it off, and you both know you still want to be together. Johnson wrote it on a plane from Miami to L.A.

J: But you came up with the hook. Teamwork.

G: I guess we're both pretty lucky in that neither of us has personally dealt with heartache or a messy breakup yet. But I know if I were dealing with it, I'd put down a sick song and that would be my release. Song writing can be your therapy.

J: I hope that when people listen to our music, they can connect to it. They can relate to the emotions we put in there. It makes sense because we're all human beings who want to feel loved and accepted. That's what's at the core.

G: That was deep. Really deep. I'm like crying right now.

AskJacks

TOP FIVE THINGS WE LOOK FOR IN A SIGNIFICANT OTHER

1. Someone who makes you laugh. You can have a good time together, be playful, be goofy. A girl who's serious all the time just brings you down.

2. Someone who makes you feel comfortable. There are no awkward silences across the table; you're not always "on" or minding your manners. You can speak your mind without being judged, and you can cut loose and she digs it.

3. Someone who's down for anything. Spontaneous, fun-loving, carefree, eager to try something new. You wanna go see the chimps in the zoo, she's up for it.

4. Someone who doesn't stress. You don't want a person who always freaks out at the slightest thing or makes you feel like you're walking on eggshells. That's just annoying.

5. Someone who gets along with your friends and family. This is huge if you're going the distance. She has to hand with the homies because they know you best—and frankly, you can't get rid of them.

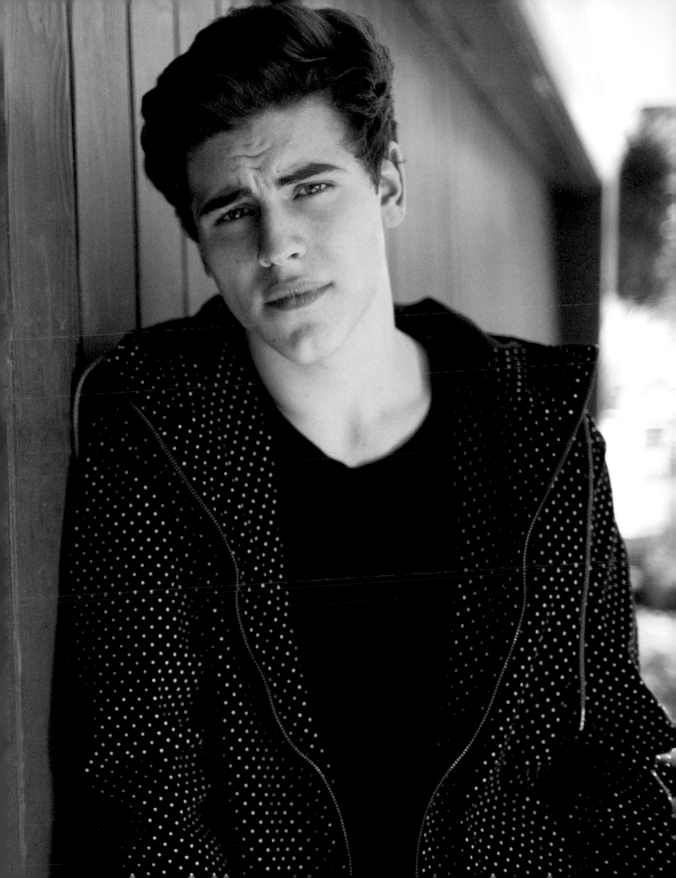

I DON'T THINK EITHER OF US WERE EVER REALLY **PLAYERS**

≪≪≪≪≪≪TMI

G: Right when we came out to L.A., we had just gotten out of year-long-plus relationships. We were like, "Let's focus. Let's not think about anything long term with girls."

J: Yeah, that lasted like a split second for him. . . .

G: Well, I met this girl, and I really liked her. It was unavoidable. I couldn't ignore my feelings. I'm really happy, and she's in this business, too, so it works really well.

J: I respect that. But I'm flyin' solo.

G: The lone wolf on the prowl. I want deets.

J: I don't think you should ever, on principle, kiss and tell. Unless it's some badass celebrity chick like Rihanna. Then you gotta brag and tell your bros. You just gotta.

G: Just know that you are probably putting it out there. You tell, and someone else will tell. It's a fact. So if you can live with that . . .

J: But sometimes you just can't keep it bottled up inside, you know? Like I would have to tell you.

G: I say if you're single, go ahead and brag about it. But if you're in a relationship . . .

J: I'd say keep it on the low.

G: He's a different kinda guy right here.

J: I don't think either of us were ever really players, though. Back in high school, we both had a few relationships, but there wouldn't be hookups with different girls every weekend. I mean, maybe the random make-out at a party.

G: Nah, we weren't players.

J: And today . . . well, I'm still single. I let girls know from the beginning that I'm not looking for a relationship. I'm not trying to break any hearts, you feel me?

G: And I'm in a relationship. So I don't have to deal with any of that. Thankfully.

J: I don't have a preference—blond or brunette or redhead. A cute girl is a cute girl.

G: Truth.

MY FIRST KISS WAS IN THE SEVENTH GRADE

«««««LIP LOCKS

J I think my first kiss was my mom.

G Aw, that's sweet. But we're talkin' lip-to-lip, blood-pumpin' emotion here.

J Oh, okay. Then my first kiss was in the summer between fifth and sixth grade in summer camp in Canada.

G Damn! You were a youngin'.

J I was, I was. My friend actually kissed the same girl—it was his first kiss, too. She was going into seventh grade. An older woman. I guess she thought we were cute. I will never forget it.

G You guys bragged about it a lot. Where did it happen?

J It was by this green lake. Seriously—it was all green with algae or something, like a swamp.

G: My first kiss was in the seventh grade, and you made it happen.

J: I did! I take full credit! You had this girlfriend and you had been dating for like a year.

G: We played tennis together at the same club—we weren't dating.

J: Okay, you were crushing. But we were all at a bar mitzvah, and I was like, "Come on, guys, you can do it. It's no biggie. It's just lip-to-lip contact." I was like the Kiss Coach.

G: 'Cause you were *so* experienced.

J: I said, "Okay, Jack, here's her hand. Just kiss her hand."

G: Then you suggested I move to the cheek. So I kissed her on the cheek.

J: Then I said, "Okay, come on, now do it on the lips.

It's just two inches to the right. It's really not that big of a deal."

G: We finally kissed. "With You" by Chris Brown was playing and that became our song. She's a nice girl, and I see her sometimes back in Omaha.

AskJacks

BOXERS OR BRIEFS?

J: Boxer-briefs. I'm a hybrid man.

G: I rock the long Ethikas. Love those.

WHAT WOULD BE YOUR DREAM DATE?

G: Me and my girlfriend, and all my dudes and their girlfriends, would go to some tropical locale and jump out of a plane. That would be really cool.

J: With parachutes, I hope? Otherwise, that is the last dream date you're goin' on.

G: Goes without saying.

J: Mine would be with Marilyn Monroe in her prime. That would probably make my life.

G: Where would you take her?

J: Dude, Marilyn Monroe. Does it matter?

G: Good point.

J: I just wanna take a selfie with her. But if it was back in the day, we'd probably go see a Frank Sinatra concert and hang backstage.

G: That would be legendary.

DO YOU WANT TO SETTLE DOWN ONE DAY? GET MARRIED AND HAVE KIDS?

G: Definitely. Of course.

J: I wanna be married before I'm thirty. I feel like it will help me focus. I don't want to be single my entire life. That stuff's

fun, but once you're past twenty-five, you know what you want and you can decide on the right partner for you.

G: Live it up till you're thirty.

J: I wanna have a kid when I'm young. I wanna be the cool dad.

G: I'll be the cool dad even when I'm eighty.

J: Yeah, you will.

WHICH ONE OF YOU IS THE BEST KISSER?

J: You'd probably have to ask a mutual make-out girl. There were a few back in high school.

G: Yeah, there are a few. We're not naming names, but if you wanted to go and investigate . . .

J: They could answer that question for you. We're not equipped.

G: I don't think I wanna know!

WHAT IS THE MOST ROMANTIC THING YOU'VE EVER DONE FOR A GIRL?

J: I'm not really a mushy-gushy kinda guy. Flowers and dinner on Valentine's Day, probably. I don't overthink or overdo it.

G: Balloons. Flowers. A big teddy bear. I'm with you on this—you don't need to make a big scene to show you care. Words. Words are romantic.

HOW DO YOU TELL SOMEONE IT'S OVER WITHOUT BREAKING HER HEART INTO A MILLION PIECES?

J: You gotta be calm. Don't be in her face. Think of how you would feel on the receiving end.

G: If you're ending it, there's a reason. Be up front about it. State it. And remember, even if the girlfriend-boyfriend thing isn't working out, you can still be friends.

J: Eventually. Give it some time. But let's be real, it'll never be the same.

CHAPTER 5

TAKE A
PASS
TURN

IF SOMEONE PRESENTS YOU WITH *AN* **OPPORTUNITY,** **TAKE IT**

EVERYONE HAS A PASSION

J: IF YOU DON'T KNOW WHAT IT IS RIGHT NOW, THEN KEEP LOOKING. IT'S OUT THERE. GET OUT AND TRY STUFF. YOU'LL NEVER FIND IT AT HOME SITTING ON YOUR COUCH.

G: THAT'S THE KEY—GIVE STUFF A CHANCE. IF SOMEONE PRESENTS YOU WITH AN OPPORTUNITY, TAKE IT, EVEN IF YOU DON'T THINK IT'S "YOUR THING." HOW DO YOU KNOW UNTIL YOU'VE GIVEN IT A SHOT?

J: And how do you know when you actually have stumbled onto something? For us, it was a gut feeling. We were getting excited and kind of obsessed over making our videos and later our music. It was all we could think about.

G: You'll know. It may start off as a hobby, but when it becomes lucrative—like hey, this could actually be my full-time job, or, like Jack says, when you can't think of anything else, then you've hit on something. And you should follow that path, because you can't ever go wrong doing something you love. You can only go wrong doing something you don't like. If it's got you fired up, then it's a sure sign.

AskJacks
WORDS THAT ARE IMPOSSIBLE TO RHYME . . . AND WE'VE TRIED!

J: Orange. Technically you could make it happen with words like *porridge* or *snorange*.

G: That's not a word.

J: I didn't say it was perfect.

G: Purple. I'm stumped on a word that rhymes with purple. Totally.

J: Inconspicuous. Ubiquitous. Discombobulate.

G: Basically, all of those SAT words you had to memorize. Un-rhymable.

J: Onomatopoeia.

G: Wait! I can do it! Onomatopoeia. Told a girl I don't wanna see her!

J: It's a stretch, but I'll take it.

TAKE ALL THAT PASSION, TURN IT INTO ACTION

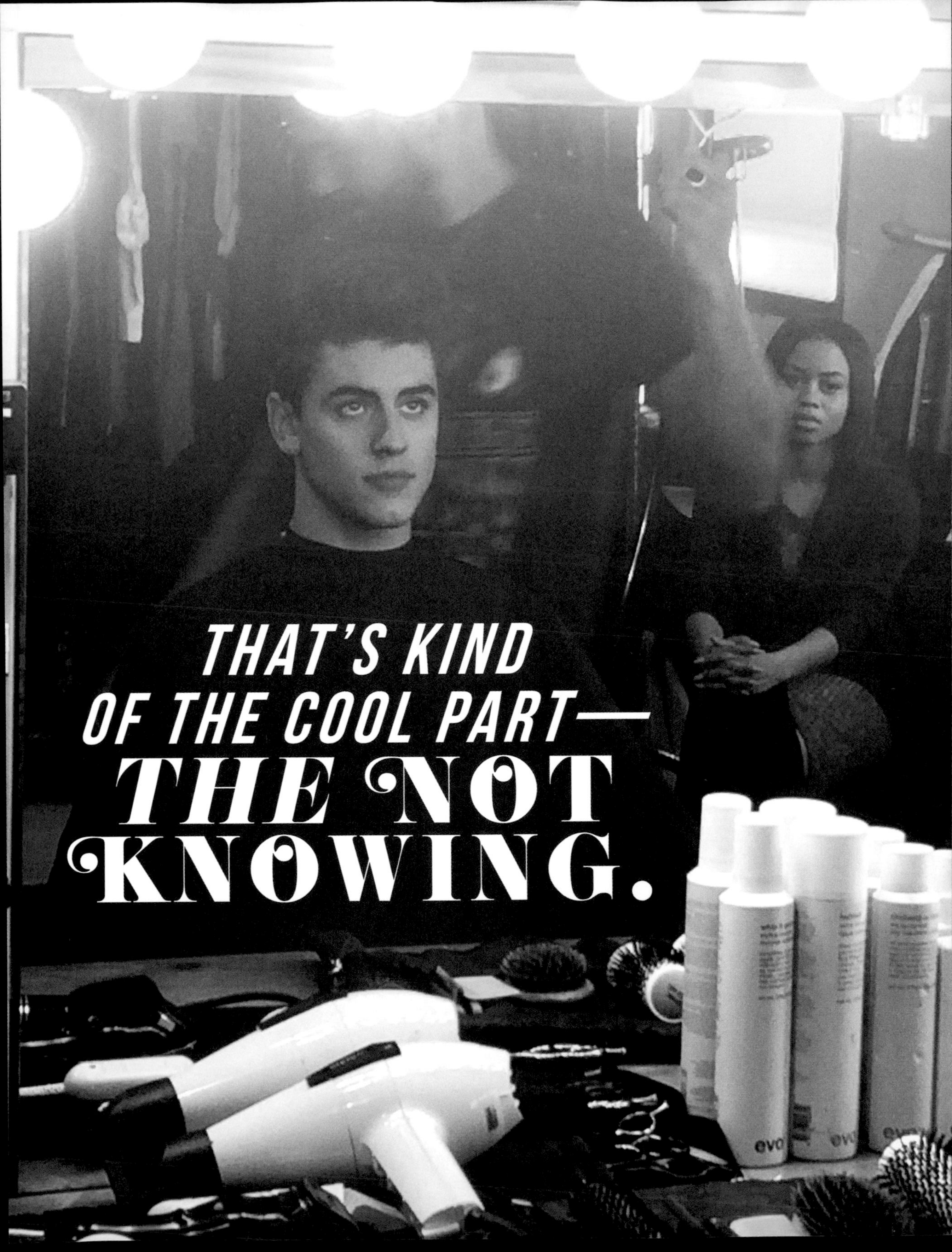

THAT'S KIND
OF THE COOL PART—
THE NOT
KNOWING.

J: Then what are you going to do to put it out there? You need a game plan. What are your dreams? Your goals? A lot of people thought we were nuts to make a career out of the Vine thing, but we began to realize it was our ticket. There's no such thing as a crazy idea if what you're doing is making people happy—and making you happy. Who's crazy now, right?

G: I don't think we had a clear vision of "We're goin' to Hollywood." It was more like "Let's put this out there and see how people respond" or "Let's throw down some tracks and see if people like them." It was a lot of trial and error, a lot of experimenting to find our sound. At some point, you have to trust it and believe in it and believe in yourself.

J: And that's kind of the cool part—the not knowing. And also realizing that something good can even come out of something bad. The old "one door closes, another opens" cliché. Failure can be a motivator, too. Don't beat yourself up if you try something and fail at it. At some point, something will stick.

G: We try a lot of stuff with our music and our videos and not everything works. It's part of the process. If you see it that way, there's no such thing as failing. Just moving toward getting it right.

AskJacks

WHO WAS THE ARTIST WHO MADE YOU WANT TO PURSUE A MUSIC CAREER?

G: For me, it was Bono. I was watching a U2 concert, and I remember thinking, I wanna be him. He could command that stage. He could move the audience.

J: For me, it was probably one of the first concerts I went to in this huge arena in Omaha: Black Eyed Peas. They put on such a cool show with all the crazy lights and the background dancers, it was such a full production. They made me wanna be a performer, get on stage and entertain people. Musically, behind the scenes, I'd have to say Lil Wayne has been a big influence on me.

CHUNKY OR SMOOTH PEANUT BUTTER?

G: Smooth. I don't even want to think about it being a peanut before.

J: Smooth. Who eats chunky? Who wants to crunch your PB and J? That's just too much work.

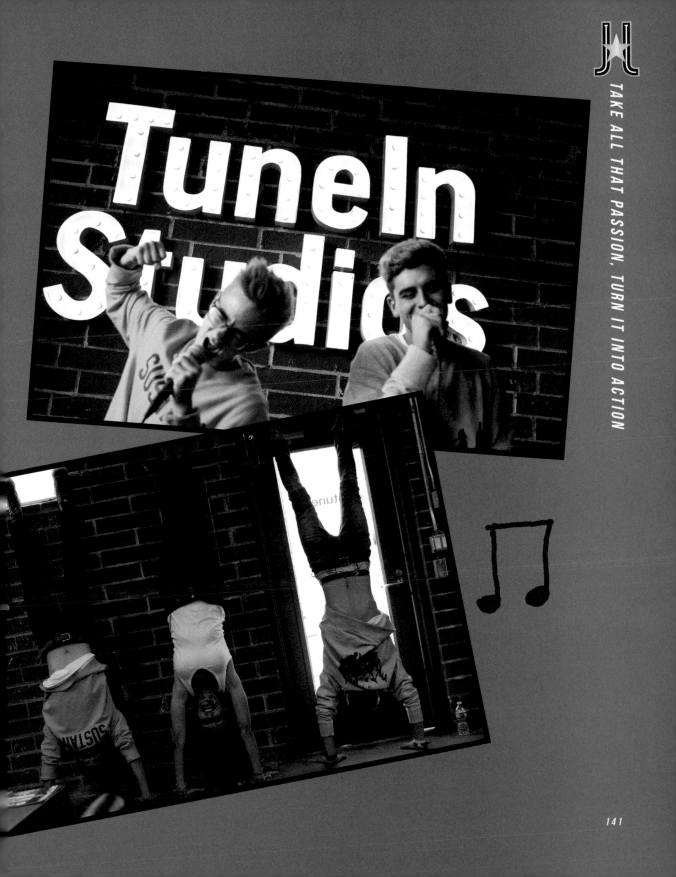

MILK OR DARK CHOCOLATE?

J: Milk. All day. Although dark is better for your health.

G: Although if you're eating chocolate, who cares? You're not doin' it for your health. Am I right?

FAVE PLACE IN THE WORLD YOU'VE BEEN AND WHY?

J: Colorado. I have so many memories of being there with my friends, skiing and snowboarding.

G: That's such a hard question! I've loved so many places we've been to, but we've only been there for a few days, so I can't make an educated choice. I guess I'd have to say California is high on the list for sure, and there's nothing like a Caribbean getaway with the family. Or maybe I'd steal Jack's and say Colorado, too.

J: Get your own, man.

FAVE CEREAL?

J: Ooh, that's tough! I'm a huge fan of Blueberry Frosted Mini-Wheats and Strawberry Frosted Mini-Wheats.

G: Mini-Wheats? You're kidding, right?

J: I'm a big fruit fan.

G: Cocoa Krispies. I know, so bad for you. But so worth it.

FAVE CANDY?

J: Sour Patch Kids—I'm a sucker for them. Or Haribo gummy bears. It's like a little hard and chewy on the outside, but the center is really soft.

G: Milk Duds with Sour Patch a close second.

J: You're stealin' my answers again.

BOOK THAT CHANGED YOUR LIFE?

G: *The Jungle Book.* Not the Disney movie. I actually read the book.

J: For me, it was *A Long Way Gone*, about a child soldier in Africa. He gets kidnapped by the rebels, and he does drugs and is forced to kill people when he's literally nine years old. It's about how he got out of all that and got to America. It's pretty powerful.

G: *Where the Red Fern Grows*. That was a sad one. I think it was our required sixth-grade read-along.

J: *The Giver*—I loved that one, too. What would society be like with no pain, no feeling at all?

G: *Hatchet*. That one really spoke to me. The wilderness . . . I was in it. I could see it; I could hear it in surround sound. For me, that's the key to a great book. You feel like you're actually in it, living it.

MOVIE THAT CHANGED YOUR LIFE?

J: *Interstellar*. Totally messes with your head.

G: *The Butterfly Effect* with Ashton Kutcher. Wow.

J: Oh my God, bro! Yes, that one makes you think like crazy.

G: It shows how the simplest event can change your life in a split second.

J: I also have to say *Shutter Island* with Leo DiCaprio. You don't know which person is nuts, and after you watch it you feel like you're going nuts.

G: Dark. Very dark.

WHAT SCARES THE CRAP OUT OF YOU?

J: Donald Trump becoming president. Truly, it gives me nightmares. I wake up in a cold sweat.

G: He might win—and that's scary as crap.

J: If he does, we're gonzo. We're Caribbean bound. So you may be reading this book years from now, and Jack & Jack are coming to you live from a desert island, sipping tropical drinks under an umbrella. Thanks to The Donald.

WHAT'S THE FUNNIEST THING YOU'VE EVER DONE?

J: I cannot think of one specific incident because Jack G's one funny dude. He's made me pee-in-pants laugh a couple of times.

G: I'm proud to have that effect on you.

J: Back in the day, before the phone, all we had were jokes and pranks. We've spent too many years together to just choose one "funniest" thing.

G: Our lives are a greatest hits of funny things. I just look at you and crack up, man.

OUR LIVES ARE A **GREATEST HITS** OF FUNNY THINGS.

J: Funny is my middle name.

G: I thought it was Edward?

IF YOU COULD PICK A DIFFERENT DECADE TO LIVE IN, WHAT WOULD YOU CHOOSE?

G: I'd wanna fast-forward to 2500 and see what the future is like.

J: Wait—what if you could go back to watching Jimi Hendrix perform live at Woodstock?

G: Ooh, I would love that. Like the seventies or sixties? Or somewhere in the middle—like 1965 to 1975. I know that's not an official decade, but it's ten years.

J: I just wanna see how the hippie movement took over the world and chilled it out, you know? Or go backstage at a Beatles concert and hang with them. All four. I think the world was at a happier, chiller place, and I'd like to experience it.

G: Would you go hippie?

J: Yeah, I might. Just to check it out, you know.

G: Flowers and stuff . . . tie-dye?

J: Maybe. I could get into it.

G: I could totally see you rockin' that look.

J: Thanks. I think.

DO YOU HAVE TATTOOS?

J: We do not. We're still bare. But we talk about it all the time.

G: We want tattoos so bad, but it's just gotta be right.

J: It's the commitment. We gotta commit to something. If we knew what that something was, it would already be there.

G: Tattoos stick with you for life, so we gotta gain some more life experiences before we make a decision. It's a big one, so we are not rushing into it. But when we do . . . it will be dope.

"WOULD YOU GO HIPPIE?" "YEAH, I MIGHT."

CHAPTER 6

NO SHOES,
SWIMT
&RAY

BALANCING WORK *AND FUN IS* EASY FOR US

STRIKING A BALANCE

J: BALANCING WORK AND FUN IS EASY FOR US, REALLY. WORK IS PLAY FOR US. MAKING MUSIC IS FUN, STRAIGHT UP.

G: I FEEL LIKE EVEN IF WE TAKE A VACATION, WE'RE GONNA END UP FINDING A STUDIO WHEREVER WE ARE AND PICK UP WHERE WE LEFT OFF. THAT'S THE BEST THING ABOUT OUR WORK; IT DOESN'T EVER FEEL LIKE a chore. We're actually excited to get up in the morning and get to work, which is a sure sign that you're doing the right thing. If life makes you excited, you're on track.

J: And we know how to chill when we need it. We shoot hoops and play water bottle toss—you do sick combos with your friends, toss it behind your back. Not to brag, but we are the half-filled champs.

G: Yeah, and that can recharge your batteries, you know? That can be good for the work. The key is to prioritize. We just did a tour for a month, and now we have two weeks at home. We need to be writing and producing music, but we also need a few days to decompress. So you make time for both, giving weight to the things you know need to happen. It's really the difference between us way back in the day and now. We're more mature; we know there are responsibilities and obligations. If we have something we need to do, we do it.

J: Do we stress out sometimes and put too much pressure on ourselves? Yeah, of course. Guilty as charged. I find myself in a constant need to create and give our fans content. We wanna see growth. We see our numbers plateauing on social media and we panic a little.

J: If we see our likes going down, we freak. We feel like we're disappointing our followers. I'm in this panic mode, "We gotta put content out there, fast!" But you can't rush it. You can't just throw something up there that's sloppy.

G: You can't rush greatness. We need to make this the best that we can, and that's when the fans will realize why it's taking so long.

J: But I still feel that stress, creeping up the back of my neck. We gotta hurry it up. We've got fans counting on us.

G: Fans first, goofing around later.

J: But a lot of our content actually comes from goofing around.

G: Right. Like I said, our work is play and our play is work. It's pretty linked.

J: You realize not many people can say that. What if we were firefighters or cops?

G: We'd have some pretty dope uniforms, that's for sure. Girls love those uniforms.

AskJacks

WHAT IS YOUR IDEA OF THE PERFECT DAY OFF?

G: I would say the beach. Get some sun, get some rays. In the summer especially. That's the place to be. Or Netflix, room service, chill.

J: But to be honest, I'd wanna be in the studio, too. It's fun as hell. I love making music, and there's no better feeling.

G: Agreed.

J: No days off, that's my mind-set.

DO YOU HAVE A TO-DO LIST?

G: I would say no. I don't have a physical list I check off. It's more mental, "Let's get work done, and we need to strategize." I keep it all in my head.

J: I'd say there are some big things, like get an album done and win a Grammy and perform on a late-night talk show. But it's more like a goals list. It will happen in time, no deadlines.

YOU CAN'T RUSH GREATNESS.

TO DO NOTHING FEELS AWFUL.

G: But you don't write it down.

J: You mean like on a Post-it? Nah. I'd probably lose it anyway.

DO YOU HAVE A MAN CAVE? DESCRIBE!

J: Yes, we do, and it's at our buddy Nash Grier's house. It's called "The Time Machine." It's a shack with these crazy posters hung everywhere, and that's where we go to listen to music and just chill with our homies. We'll bring our snacks in there and just have a good time.

G: It has these lights that change. It's really cool. We'll play our new tunes in there for our friends and hang. It's like our escape from the world.

J: Every dude should have a man cave. Women should have a woman cave.

G: How do you know they don't?

J: 'Cause no one invites a guy into a woman cave.

G: Speak for yourself.

WHEN WAS THE LAST TIME YOU DID NOTHING?

J: I don't know. Wait! I lie, I do. Remember when me and Nash were just playing video games for like two weeks straight?

G: I do. January 2015.

J: We were on a video game binge, and we would just order in food to be delivered. We didn't leave my house once. It was like we were hibernating.

G: I would come back to the house every day to change and shower, and you guys would be in the same place, the same position, a little greasier, maybe more pizza boxes and Chinese takeout boxes piled up, but still in the same spot. You even had one of those Edible Arrangements of fruit—like a bouquet made out of strawberries and pineapples?

J: It kind of pissed me off later; it was the most unproductive two weeks of my life.

G: We went a few months like that when we first got out here, where we weren't going into the studio. We look back now and it sucked.

J: Exactly. To do nothing feels awful. I hate it. I hate to be stagnant.

G: I think it has to happen when you first come out to L.A. You need to hang and party, and then you realize it's time to get down to business. You see how productive you can be, and you don't want to be lazy anymore.

ARE YOU WORKAHOLICS OR PLAYAHOLICS?

J: Definitely workaholics. I just want to be working every day.

G: When we're not touring, meeting fans, playing concerts, we're in the studio. And that's not gonna stop for a long time. We've got goals we wanna hit, and hard work is the only way to make them happen.

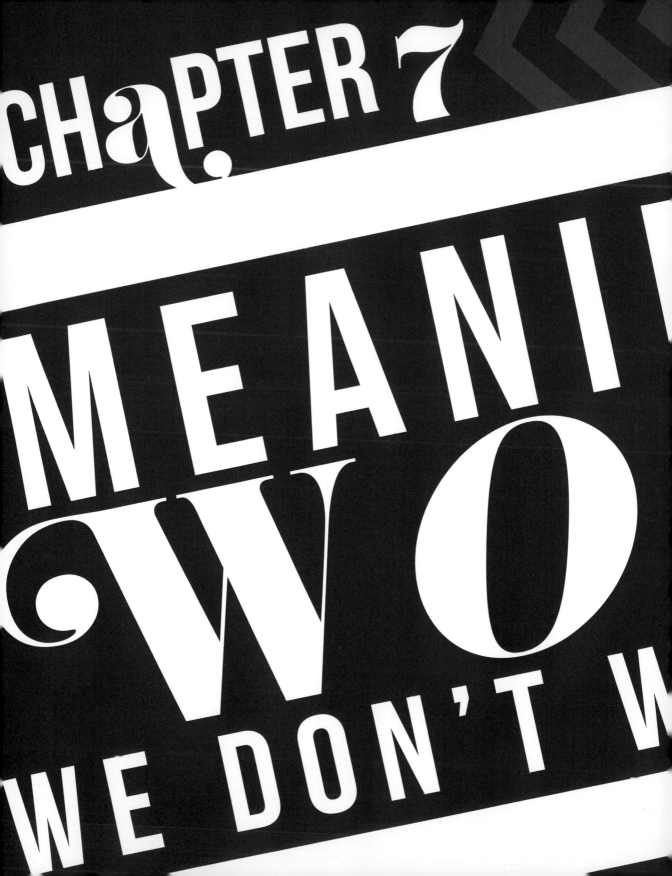

CHAPTER 7

MEANI
WO
WE DON'T W

HANDLING THE HATERS

J: WHEN WE FIRST STARTED OUT, IT WASN'T EASY. WE'D READ THE HATE COMMENTS AND IT WOULD GET TO US. PEOPLE WOULD BE LIKE, "VINE? SIX-SECOND VIDEOS? YOU GUYS PROBABLY LAST SIX SECONDS IN BED . . ."

G: OH YEAH. I REMEMBER THAT ONE. AND YA THINK YOU'RE SO CLEVER, DUDE . . .

J: LOTS OF CHEESY LITTLE JOKES AND LAME DIGS MEANT TO HURT US.

G: They ripped us apart, but that was expected. We knew clearly not everyone was gonna love us.

J: Which isn't to say it didn't sting. No one likes to hear negative things. No one likes to be knocked down. But you have to ask yourself, where is this coming from? Is it jealousy? Is it insecurity? Are you putting your own bad feelings about yourself on someone else to build yourself up? Is that gonna make your misery go away—to make someone else miserable?

G: Bad strategy. It actually makes you look smaller. And that's what we remind ourselves: Consider the source when someone hates on you.

J: Pity the source.

G: Exactly. You hate yourself, so you're gonna hate on someone else? That's pretty transparent.

J: You can't control the person who is putting those negative comments out there, but you can control your reaction. You can rise above it, you know? You can keep it in perspective. What does what this person have to say that really matters? Am I gonna let it

AskJacks

NOTES TO THE HATERS

"JACK & JACK LOL! AREN'T THEY THOSE KIDS FROM VINE?
WTF ARE THEY DOING IN MUSIC? THIS IS WHACK!"

First of all, we're not from Vine, we're from Nebraska.
And second of all, I don't think Vine has anything to do
with how talented an individual is. Getting noticed on Vine
takes skill—so thanks for pointing it out.

"JACK J. LOOKS LIKE HE'S TWELVE AND A PARROT JUST
POOPED ON HIM . . ."

I know I look like I'm twelve, but I'm not. I was born in
1996. I'm out here living my dreams, so the fact that
you're taking time to comment on my looks is a little
suspect. Maybe you should get a pet parrot to keep you
company?

"ALL YOUR SONGS AND VINES SUCK."

A hater is just a fan who's scared to admit it. If you're
obsessing over "all" our music and Vines, then obviously
we made ya look and listen. We'll make sure to put out a
bunch more for you. Wouldn't want to disappoint.

bring me down, or am I gonna keep on doing what I'm doing, what makes me happy?

G: I remind myself these people have nothing better to do with their lives than watch my Vines and post nasty comments. That's pathetic, but hey, thanks for tuning in.

J: Haters are great free promo.

G: If someone's hating on you, just put your situation next to theirs. You'll feel a lot better.

J: It doesn't matter what you do, chances are there will always be some lame person who finds fault in it, who judges you. Don't let them push your buttons. Be bigger and better than that.

G: And hit delete. Or walk away. Best defense is not to get defensive. Give it the attention it deserves: none.

J: Remember that it's easy to attract haters. All you have to do is be confident, talented, good looking, opinionated, smart . . . you get what I'm saying? If you've got haters, you're doing something right.

AskJacks

YOUR FRIEND HAS FOOD STUCK IN HIS TEETH. DO YOU TELL HIM?

J: Oh yeah. With one of our homies, I'd just say: "Dude, there's some spinach hangin' out there. . . ."

G: It's not like you're on a date with some girl and you gotta be smooth. You just tell him, so that if a pretty girl does come along, he's all good.

J: I would wanna be told.

G: The one thing I'm iffy on telling someone is the booger thing.

J: That is a little uncomfortable.

G: I mean, I would tell you.

J: I would hope so.

G: But it's just like, when there's a bat in the cave, I don't wanna look at it and I certainly don't wanna talk about it.

WHERE DOES ALL YOUR CONFIDENCE COME FROM, AND CAN YOU LEND ME SOME?

G: I think it comes from the fans, because they've been so supportive.

J: I feel like any time of the day, Jack and I can just go pop in on our Twitter or Instagram and see the comments and feel the love. That's a huge confidence booster to us. Even if I'm like, "I feel like a piece of crap today," that elevates me.

G: Always.

J: I mean, look at this comment on my Twitter: "Hope you have a great day! I love you!!!"

G: Three exclamation points. That is impressive. That is confidence boosting. Sometimes for me, it's just seeing the numbers: there are 4.1 million people who care what I have to post today. It's an amazing feeling.

J: Beyond that, I'd say we believe in ourselves and our dreams, as cheesy as that sounds. But that's what gives us confidence. The feeling that we are following our dreams and making them happen.

G: If you ever get down on yourself, just know that there are people out there who appreciate you for who you are.

J: You just gotta find those people and keep them close. It could be your mom or your dog, and that's all you need. Right there you have someone who's got your back.

WOULD ERIC AND WINSTON EVER TEAM UP ON A HATERS SONG? NERDS UNITE!

G: Great idea—and we love us those nerds—but I don't think that we would ever make a song that was a joke. Unless maybe we were on *Saturday Night Live*.

J: Our music is the one thing that is never a joke. We might have a goofy lyric here or there, but we take it really serious and keep it really separate from Nerd Vandals and the comedy. But then you never know, if we blow up—fingers

crossed—and *SNL* comes to us, we'll keep that idea in mind.

G: Never say never.

DO YOU READ ALL THE REVIEWS AND THE COMMENTS PEOPLE WRITE ABOUT YOU—OR DO YOU IGNORE THEM?

J: I'll read what people comment, absolutely. Usually the top comments when we post a new Vine, for example, because I want to see if people got a chuckle out of it.

G: I probably read the original music—related comments the most. We work so hard on our music content, and we love the feedback. I try to read as many comments as possible on the regular socials, and I try and ignore the haters; there's just not enough time for them.

J: The music is what we work hard on and take seriously, and we value the constructive criticism and feedback from the fans on it.

CHAPTER 8

THE WORL

PL
GRO

GOING GLOBAL

J: WE NEVER EXPECTED TO HAVE FANS ALL OVER THE WORLD, OUTSIDE OF OUR COUNTRY. IT'S JUST CRAZY. BUT THAT JUST SHOWS THE POWER OF SOCIAL MEDIA. EVERYTHING IS INSTANTLY INTERNATIONAL THESE DAYS. THERE'S NO SLOW DIFFUSION INTO FOREIGN COUNTRIES, WE'RE THERE. THEY SEE US AND THEY KNOW US.

WE'RE JUST HAPPY TO BE HERE.

G: We've been to Canada, South America, Australia, New Zealand, the UK, and all over Europe. I feel like we've seen almost all of Europe at this point. Can we just take a moment here: Nebraska to New Zealand. How did this happen? Our lives, man . . .

J: Do you have a fave spot we've been?

G: I would say the fans in South America have a level up on everybody else. They tear the roof down, you know?

J: Barcelona was beautiful. Scenic-wise, it blew me away.

G: We'll get maybe a day or two in a city, so it's really hard to say, "This one was the best." We've loved it all, every minute of it. Playing to live audiences especially.

J: And we are the most chill people when it comes to our concerts. Some acts have a mile-long list in their contracts about what they will and won't do, what they must have in their dressing rooms. Like green M&Ms only, bottles of Dom, and the room has to be eighty-seven degrees or else.

G: Us? We're like, "Just give us some water and a fruit plate, a pot of tea." Maybe some steam. Is that being a diva?

J: You gotta keep the pipes warmed up, ya know? Sometimes you got phlegm.

G: Did you just say phlegm?

J: I did. I am not ashamed. But I'm not sure I can spell it.

G: We're very low maintenance. We're just happy to be here.

❮❮❮❮❮❮ BUCKLE YOUR SEAT BELTS

J: I know we just said we're low maintenance, but if we're on an international flight and it's a long one, we fly first-class 'cause we've gotta get our sleep for the show the next day.

THE WORLD IS OUR PLAYGROUND

WE'RE VERY **LOW MAINTENANCE.**

G: And that's really our call if we want to spend the money on it—it's not like, "Oh, we're big shots. We need to be in first." It's really about being practical and getting a good night's rest. Coach is cramped, and then we're jet-lagged.

J: And he is ugly when he's jet-lagged.

G: No sleep on a twelve-hour flight? Yeah, you bet I'm ugly.

J: But anything less than a five-hour flight, we'll chill in coach. We're not big spenders. We save our money for a rainy day, you know? On the American tour, we haven't taken any planes. It's all buses. Hit the road, Jacks!

G: The best part of touring is you meet so many fans and you gain fans. Performing live is the most exhilarating experience. And you make friends around the world—it's crazy, we have friends in Dublin, Amsterdam, and London now!

J: The worst part is staying on a consistent schedule: sleeping, eating, working out. Your body just starts to

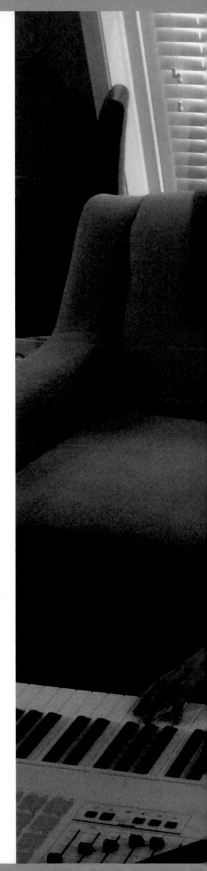

break down sometimes and you're like, "I can't keep up with this."

G: You wake up in a new time zone and the jet lag is brutal. You lose hours or gain hours and your body has no idea what time it is anymore.

J: I hate that. I hate when it's like the middle of the night and I'm ready for breakfast.

G: So you just have to keep yourself moving, force yourself to eat or stay awake on the local time, when your brain is screaming, "Are you out of your freakin' mind?"

J: But then you play to the crowds and it energizes you. Makes it all worthwhile.

G: The biggest crowd we've ever played was a festival in NYC—twenty-five thousand people. But we never really

AS SOON AS I GET OUT THERE . . . .
I'M PUMPED.
I'M IN THE ZONE.

think about the numbers or get nervous.

J: Nah, we're perfectly comfortable. They're our fans. Now if we opened for a big band . . .

G: Right, and they sold like 90 per cent of the tickets? Then I'd be kinda nervous. 'Cause they're not there for us. They may not even know us.

J: In any case though, as soon as I get out there . . . I'm pumped. I'm in the zone.

G: Doesn't matter if you speak our language or not, you're showin' us the love and we're feelin' it.

AskJacks

WHAT IS YOUR FAVE SONG TO PERFORM LIVE?

G: "Like That" is mine.

J: Mine I would say right now is this mashup of Fetty Wap's "Again" and Bob Marley's "One Love." I have this really cool rap that I wrote and none of the fans know it, so they gotta listen and it catches them off guard. And I play keys at the end, which has really helped me get comfortable playing piano on stage.

HAVE YOU EVER SCREWED UP ON STAGE AND COVERED IT UP?

J: Um, yeah. All the time.

G: I got a nosebleed once. I fell off the stage. I could go on and on. There's always something that's going to go wrong during a show. No show is ever perfect, and I think that's what makes a perfect show—how you deal with it.

J: How you handle the flaws and bounce back without missing a beat.

G: You never know when a girl is gonna throw a bracelet and it hits you in the face mid high note.

J: Wait, that happened?

G: Oh yeah. But it was an accident, she was waving her hands in the air like she just don't care.

J: Literally, something happens every show. But I don't think there's ever been a crazy moment where we've stopped in our tracks. We roll with it. We know how to play it off.

G: Right, no awkward pauses or silences. Maybe if I was alone on stage I wouldn't be as relaxed about it, but I know that if I screw it up, I can look over at Jack and he's there to cover for me. No matter what, there's one of us to fill the gap.

J: We jam off each other.

CAN YOU ACTUALLY SEE ME SCREAMING IN THE AUDIENCE AND WAVING MY SIGN OR AM I JUST WASTING MY TIME?

J: Honestly, we probably can see you. A lot depends on the venue size of course, but on the US run we did, with 1,000 to 1,500 average in the audience, I can see every face out there. I can pick you out.

G: We don't have our own lighting guys, so it doesn't even get dark in the venue. I see everyone's faces for sure.

J: Sometimes we'll just stop the show and start reading signs out loud.

G: Keep holding 'em up, because we see you guys and it warms our hearts.

WHO DO YOU PREFER—BEATLES OR STONES?

J: I'm a Beatles guy—no disrespect to the Stones. But I feel like their music was so innovative, deep, and thoughtful.

G: And I feel like the Stones are the ultimate party band. Rock stars, 100 percent.

WE SEE YOU GUYS AND
IT WARMS
OUR HEARTS.

J: I personally regard Paul and John as two of the best writers of all time. Stones have sick melodies, don't get me wrong. But I'm just into the Beatles's vibe more.

WHAT ARE THREE ADJECTIVES YOU WOULD USE TO DESCRIBE EACH OTHER?

J: Organized, funny, persistent. That's you.

G: Messy, intelligent . . . and genuine.

J: I'll take it.

CHAPTER 9

A DAY
IN
LIFE

TYPICAL DAY

J: SO, WHAT'S A TYPICAL DAY IN OUR LIFE LIKE? HONESTLY, THERE IS NOTHING TYPICAL ABOUT IT. WE CAN'T EVER SAY WE DO THE SAME THING AT THE SAME TIME EVERY DAY. WHATEVER'S GOING ON TODAY MAY BE TOTALLY DIFFERENT TOMORROW.

G: IT SOUNDS COOL TO BE SO SPONTANEOUS, BUT SOMETIMES WE DO WISH WE HAD MORE OF A SCHEDULE GOING ON. WE TRY, BUT SOMETHING ALWAYS COMES UP.

J: WE'VE GOTTEN REALLY GOOD AT ROLLING WITH THINGS.

SLEEPING ON THE TOUR BUS!

WE'RE THE

LOOKING GOOD

READY, SET . . .

REHEARSALS

BIG DECISIONS

GETTING LOOSE

WARMING UP

SHOWTIME!

WOULD YOU RATHER . . .

EAT FRENCH FRIES OR TATER TOTS?

J: Fries.

G: Fries all the way.

HAVE BAGELS OR TOAST?

J: Bagels for the both of us. New York bagels in particular.

USE KETCHUP OR MUSTARD?

G: Ketchup. Goes on everything.

WEAR SNEAKERS OR GO BAREFOOT?

J: Barefoot is nice, but it's a summer thing.

G: Yeah, sneakers cover all weather, all seasons. Gotta be practical about that.

HAVE A STOMACH BUG FOR A DAY OR LARYNGITIS FOR A WEEK?

J: I hate throwing up. I mean I really hate it. There's nothing worse.

G: Yeah, but it's one day and you're over it. What if you couldn't talk for a week?

J: It would suck, but I could text. Or maybe whisper?

G: Laryngitis seems like more of a commitment, though. So I'd go for the throwing up.

WHAT'S SOMETHING NO ONE KNOWS ABOUT EACH OF YOU?

G: I get to take this one first.

J: Oh boy, here we go.

G: So recently, we were in London at this club. Let me just preface this by saying eighteen is the legal drinking age there. So Johnson has this glass of champagne in his hand.

J: I do not recall any of this, so don't hold it against me.

G: So he takes the glass, takes a sip, then turns to me and says, "Hey, check this out." Then he throws it at the wall and the glass shatters in a million pieces.

J: And your point is?

G: My point is no one knows that you are reckless.

J: I admit it:Sometimes, I can be reckless. I'll just unleash.

OUR TOP FIVE PET PEEVES

1. Slow drivers. Come on, put some pedal to the metal! Why is it that just when you're trying to get somewhere fast you get stuck behind one of them on the freeway?

2. People who chew with their mouth open. Thanks, but I don't need to see what you're having for lunch. So annoying—and even worse when accompanied by sloppy sounds.

3. People who scrape their dinner plates with a fork. Sets our teeth on edge. Have some dignity; leave a crumb or two.

4. People who have phlegm in their throats and don't clear it. Ugh! Cough it up, dude. You sound like Darth Vader.

5. When people twist your words. Okay, so you're totally ignoring what I just said and manipulating it to fit your own agenda? People who do this are either: a) looking to pick a fight, or b) don't care what your opinion is. Just walk away.

WISH ONE:
WORLD
PEACE.

I seem like a really mild-mannered guy, but I can lose it. Now my turn?

G: Go for it.

J: One time in eighth grade Jack G purposely lost his voice. I'd lost mine and he wanted to match me. So we were standing outside a Krispy Kreme, and he says, "I just wanna see what it would be like." So he starts singing punk rock, screaming this death metal for forty-five straight minutes. And it worked.

G: Yeah, it's why my voice is deeper today. Permanent punk-rock damage.

J: Serves you right.

IF A GENIE GRANTED YOU THREE WISHES, WHAT WOULD THEY BE?

J: Wish one: world peace. I'd wish that nobody had hatred in their souls toward other human beings.

G: Beautiful. Wish two: an end to world hunger.

J: Wish three: cure all diseases. I would honestly not waste a single wish on myself when there is so much that needs to be fixed about the world we live in.

G: What would we wish for anyway? Materialistic stuff?

J: Right, and another upside—besides making the world a better place—is that people would be really grateful. We'd be legends. We just cured cancer with a wish.

G: Win-win.

DO YOU COLLECT ANYTHING?

J: Back in the day, I used to collect baseball cards and Pokémon cards. Now I have this personal collection in my head of all these water brands that I've tried. I think I'm at 278.

G: Yeah, he does. Seriously, he's always trying water—as if it tastes different. It's water.

J: It does. It's very subtle sometimes, but it does.

G: I don't collect anything.

J: Yeah you do. You collect memories from around the world.

IF YOU HAD UNLIMITED MONEY, WHAT WOULD YOU BUY?

G: Unlimited? Like it never stops pouring out of my wallet? A jumbo jet for sure.

J: A mansion on both coasts and one in Colorado. And I'd give money to every charity in the world. Cancer research? You need $200 billion? Done!

G: I don't think I would spend forty-eight hours in one place ever. I would have two drivers, on twelve-hour shifts, to take me places.

J: While your jet is fueling up—that works. See the world. I want a personal chef. Damn, everything would be so easy!

G: I think I would tip someone $500,000 just for the hell of it. Thanks for the coffee, have a great day. You deserve it.

WHAT IS YOUR MANTRA?

J: Mine is "Stay hydrated." But then I want to add, "Stay humble, stay true." Not necessarily in that order, but all important.

G: "Be who you are and who you always were." Don't change regardless of what's changing around you.

J: My favorite quote is from Bob Marley, and I like that for a mantra, too: "When it rains, some people get wet, but others feel the rain."

G: It's all about perspective, isn't it?

J: Everything is deeper than what appears on the surface—that's what it means to me.

G: "Music is great because when it hits you, you feel no pain." That's Marley as well. Or "Let's get together and feel all right." Doesn't that say it all? So simple. Why doesn't everyone just do that? Just hang out and have fun and respect each other?

EVERYTHING IS **DEEPER** THAN WHAT APPEARS ON THE SURFACE

<<<<<<ONLY IN MY DREAMS

G: I used to have this reoccurring night terror for months when I was a kid, then it just stopped. I was in my house, and it was me and my sisters and we're all alone in the kitchen making grilled cheese.

J: You cooking in the kitchen? That is scary.

G: We hear this knock on the door—a loud pounding. My parents aren't home and we're freaking out, but we open the door.

J: Why? I mean why not just keep it locked with the chain on?

G: 'Cause it's my creepy nightmare, that's why. So there are these guys standing there and they have no mouths and no eyes. Like faceless guys with just skin where the openings should be.

J: Then what?

G: Nothing. They didn't do anything, we were just scared.

J: Okay, my nightmare is scarier. There was this poodle that I loved.

G: Wait, your poodle is gonna try and top my faceless dudes?

J: It gets better. We're at my old house in the driveway, and I'm four or five and in love with this with poodle. And in my nightmare, she ends up getting killed somehow. I woke up in tears, sobbing my heart out. My mom came in and tried to comfort me, but I was a wreck. So the next day she had me draw a picture of the poodle to help the grieving process.

G: Did it?

J: Not really. But it was a really nice poodle drawing.

G: I have a lot of lucid dreams. I dream in color.

J: Oh, me too. I don't get people who dream in black-and-white. You're missing out.

G: I can literally direct my dream to go the way I want it to.

YOUR POODLE
IS GONNA TRY AND TOP MY FACELESS DUDES?

J: I've had a dream where I was in bed and I stood up and watched myself sleeping. I pulled myself up and through the roof and started flying over my city. I could go anywhere I wanted, wake anybody up that I wanted, and say, "What's good?"

G: You didn't wake me up, right? Because I need my sleep.

J: I knew it was a dream, and I was totally self-aware. I felt like I could do anything, get away with anything.

G: One time I realized I was having a dream about driving a car—and I just made myself hop out because the traffic was bad.

J: Now that's convenient. I gotta remember that.

CHAPTER 10

NE
LOOKIN

FAST-FORWARD

G: WE LIVE IN THE DAY-TO-DAY, THAT'S FOR SURE, BUT THAT DOESN'T MEAN WE AREN'T ALWAYS THINKING ABOUT THE FUTURE. FIVE YEARS FROM NOW, TEN YEARS . . . WE TALK ABOUT IT ALL THE TIME. A GOAL OF MINE IS TO BECOME A MAINSTREAM, A-LIST ARTIST, A HOUSEHOLD NAME. AND I WANNA INSPIRE PEOPLE. I'D LOVE TO HAVE SOMEONE TELL ME, AN UP-AND-COMING ARTIST, THAT I GAVE HIM OR HER THE COURAGE TO GO OUT THERE AND DO IT, TOO.

J: Five years from now, we want to still be making our music. Maybe dabbling in the acting game, too. Five years sounds like it's far away, but it's really, really close. I'll be twenty-four. Hopefully we're at stadium status.

G: Ten years from now—more business ventures. As a thirty-year-old? Investing in food franchises, apps. And farther down the road from that . . .

J: Like when we're eighty-year-old dudes.

G: I hope I make it there!

J: We will. We'll be on an island in the Caribbean, Bora-Bora, chillin'.

G: Givin' off good vibes, strumming a banjo all day long.

J: Sounds good to me.

IF YOU'RE JUST YOURSELF, THEN IT'S ALL GOOD.

≪≪≪≪≪THE KEY TO SUCCESS

G: People are always asking us, "So how did you do it? What's your secret? How can I be the next Jack & Jack?"

J: It's being authentic. I know we say that a lot, but it's the truth. People see through BS easily. If you're just yourself, then it's all good. You can't be the next Jack & Jack, 'cause you're you. Own it.

G: Exactly. Everything you do has to come from your passion, from your heart.

J: You gotta work at it, too. You can't sit back and think it will happen. What you put into it, you get out. That said, you gotta be in the right place at the right time. So add in luck to that equation, too.

G: Sounds like a Nerd Vandals equation.

J: Authenticity + Hard Work + A Little Bit of Luck = Success.

G: Ya got a Sharpie? I wanna write that down.

AskJacks

IF THERE WAS ONE MOMENT YOU COULD PRESS REPLAY ON YOUR LIVES AND PLAY OVER AGAIN AND AGAIN, WHAT WOULD IT BE?

J: Probably our sold-out international tours. I'd love to live that again.

G: Yeah, that stuff's been crazy. The last six months touring live blew us away.

J: We've seen so many people, from so many different cultures, showing us the love. And we've seen the world, places we'd never been in our lives.

G: I do feel that if you asked us this question six months from now, though, the answer would probably be releasing our first album and seeing the wild response we get from the fans.

J: I think the goal is to keep creating moments you want to replay, you know?

G: Absolutely. Keep the highs coming.

AUTHENTICITY + HARD WORK + A LITTLE BIT OF LUCK = SUCCESS

WHAT'S ON YOUR BUCKET LIST?

G: In no specific order: I want to skydive, smoke a blunt with Snoop Dogg . . .

J: When you're of age—and it's legal in the US.

G: Goes without saying, Mom.

J: Go scuba diving in the Great Barrier Reef in Australia. Be in a movie with Leo DiCaprio. Even if I'm just an extra in the background, that would be cool. I'll shine his shoes, you know?

G: Grow a beard. It's so important in my life.

J: Have a platinum album. A diamond album! Sickest thing ever.

G: I'd say that's a good list. Doable, right?

J: Totally.

IF YOU COULD TRADE PLACES WITH ONE PERSON FOR ONE DAY, WHO WOULD YOU CHOOSE?

J: Leo DiCaprio on the day he won his Oscar. Sick.

G: Maybe Jay-Z. That would be kinda cool, too.

J: Yeah, a) Beyoncé's your wife, and b) I think it would be interesting to be a different race for a day. It would broaden your wisdom and understanding.

G: Leo D. and Jay-Z. Two good ones.

WHAT DO YOU HATE MOST IN THIS WORLD?

J: Terrorists. I don't hate many things, but ISIS is up there.

G: I just hate fish. I hate the smell and I can't eat it—unless it's sushi.

J: Sushi is fish. Raw fish.

G: I know, but it doesn't really look like fish—it's wrapped up in rice and all.

J: That makes no sense.

G: Okay, I hate regret. I hate the feeling of wishing I could go back and do it differently. I wish there was no guilt and regret in this world.

WHAT'S THE GREATEST GIFT SOMEONE COULD GIVE YOU?

J: Their time. It means more than anything material. Don't get me wrong: I'll take the Rolls-Royce if you're gifting it. . . .

G: Something tangible is okay, but you can throw it away.

J: True. Your time is the most precious thing you can give us. Giving us your attention, your focus, your wisdom . . . can't top that.

IF THE WORLD WAS ENDING AND YOU COULD MAKE ONE LAST SIX-SECOND VINE, WHAT WOULD IT BE?

J: Peace out, y'all. Thanks to our families, our friends, our fans for being there, always.

G: We love you. Peace. Then fade to black.